34880000823844
BOOK CHARGING CARD

Accession No. _____ Call No. 977.4
CRA

Author *Creats, Rennay*

Title *Michigan*

Date

977.4
CRA

MICHIGAN

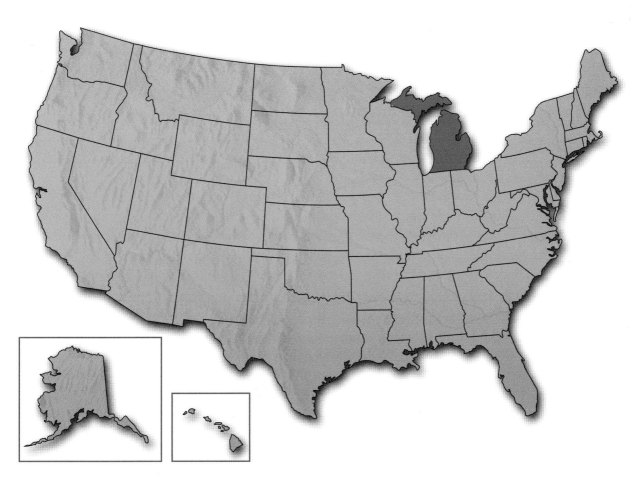

Rennay Craats

Published by Weigl Publishers Inc.
123 South Broad Street, Box 227
Mankato, MN 56002
USA
Web site: http://www.weigl.com

Library of Congress Cataloging-in-Publication Data available upon request from the publisher. Fax: (507) 388-2746 for the attention of the Publishing Records Department.

ISBN 1-930954-64-6

Printed in the United States of America
1 2 3 4 5 6 7 8 9 10   05 04 03 02 01

Editor
Jennifer Nault
Copy Editor
Jared Keen
Designers
Warren Clark
Terry Paulhus
Layout
Bryan Pezzi
Photo Researcher
Diana Marshall

Photograph Credits

Every reasonable effort has been made to trace ownership and to obtain permission to reprint copyright material. The publishers would be pleased to have any errors or omissions brought to their attention so that they may be corrected in subsequent printings.

Cover: robot arm welding car engine (Corbis Corporation), Lake Superior (Steve Mulligan Photography); **Art of Photography by Michael Jackson:** pages 4B, 5T, 5BL, 11ML; **Corbis Corporation:** page 9BL; **Corel Corporation:** pages 4BL, 14T, 14BL, 16BL, 22T, 29; **Digital Stock Corporation:** page 28B; **Ford Motor Company:** pages 4T, 13T, 28T; **Felecia Hunt-Taylor/Courtesy of Charles H. Wright MAAH:** page 22B; **Indiana Department of Natural Resources:** page 20B; **Mickey Jones/Courtesy of Travel Michigan:** page 6T; **David Kenyon, Michigan Department of Natural Resources:** pages 8T, 8BL, 10B, 11T, 11B, 18B; **D. Macmillan/Bruce Bennett Studios:** page 27B; **Raymond J. Malace/Courtesy of Travel Michigan:** page 12T; **Marquette Country Convention & Visitor Bureau:** page 20T; **Michigan Library & Historical Center:** pages 16T, 16BR, 17B, 18T, 19T, 19B; **Steve Mulligan Photography:** pages 7B, 12BL; **National Archives of Canada:** page 17T (C-98232); **Terry W. Phipps/Courtesy of Travel Michigan:** page 12BR; **PhotoDisc, Inc.:** page 13BL; **Photofest:** pages 24T, 24BR, 25T, 25B, 27T; **PhotoSpin, Inc.:** page 27BL; **Todd Rosenberg/Courtesy of Kellogg's Cereal City:** page 15B; **Don Simonelli/Courtesy of Travel Michigan:** page 10T; **Carl Ter Haar/Courtesy of Travel Michigan:** page 8BR; **Courtesy of Travel Michigan:** pages 3T, 3M, 3B, 6B, 7BL, 9T, 9BR, 13BR, 14BR, 20BL, 21T, 21B, 23T, 23BL, 23BR, 24BL, 26T, 26B; **Compliments of University Relations/Michigan State University:** page 15T.

CONTENTS

One-fifth of Michigan's total value in manufacturing comes directly from car manufacturing firms.

INTRODUCTION

The next time you are sitting in an automobile, think of Michigan. Although Michigan's official nickname is "The Wolverine State," most people associate it with its informal nickname—"The Auto State." Since the early 1900s, Michigan has been the location of incredible automotive breakthroughs. In 1903, Henry Ford established the Ford Motor Company in Detroit. There, he designed the Model T, an automobile that was more affordable than others available at the time. Demand for the Model T was high. Soon, Detroit was manufacturing so many automobiles that it earned the nickname, "Motor City."

The economic recession of the 1980s and competition with foreign car makers led to layoffs and fewer sales. Still, Michigan, along with the entire United States auto industry, bounced back. The three largest automobile manufacturers in the nation—Chrysler, General Motors, and Ford—continue to be Michigan's major employers.

QUICK FACTS

Michigan is known as "The Wolverine State" because of the importance of wolverine pelts during the early fur trading years. Another popular nickname, "The Great Lakes State," refers to these large bodies of water.

Michigan was named after Lake Michigan. It is believed that the lake's name was taken from the Algonquian word *michigama*, which means "big water."

The Detroit Metro Airport handles about 35 million passengers per year.

Getting There

Michigan is one of the Great Lakes states that make up the country's northern border. It is almost completely surrounded by water and is shaped like a mitten. Michigan is made up of two **peninsulas**—the Upper and Lower Peninsulas. Lake Superior forms the northern border of the Upper Peninsula. The Saint Mary's River makes up the eastern border, and lakes Huron and Michigan and the Straits of Mackinac form the southern boundary. Wisconsin serves as the western border.

The Lower Peninsula shares a border with Ohio and Indiana to the south and Lake Michigan to the west. To the north are lakes Huron and Michigan and the Straits of Mackinac.

There are about 121,482 miles of highways in the state. Travelers can also board a plane and land at one of nearly 460 airports in the state. The Detroit Metro Airport, the busiest airport in the state, is the eighth-busiest airport in the country.

QUICK FACTS

Although Detroit is Michigan's largest city, Lansing is the state capital.

Gerald R. Ford International Airport in Grand Rapids is Michigan's second-busiest airport.

Detroit is linked to Windsor, Ontario, Canada, by a tunnel. Bridges also connect the two countries at Sault Ste. Marie, Detroit, and Port Huron.

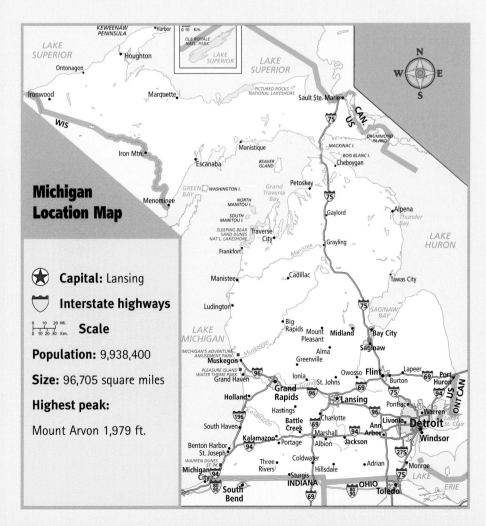

Michigan Location Map

⭐ **Capital:** Lansing

🛡 **Interstate highways**

Scale

Population: 9,938,400

Size: 96,705 square miles

Highest peak:

Mount Arvon 1,979 ft.

The Sleeping Bear Dunes rise 460 feet above Lake Michigan.

Whether natural or man-made, Michigan has some tall landmarks. A distinctive building in Detroit called the Renaissance Center towers seventy-three stories above the ground. In the 1970s, the Renaissance Center was built to breathe life into Detroit's downtown core. This complex contains retail stores, office spaces, a theater, and a hotel.

Even nature is tall in Michigan. The Sleeping Bear Dunes National Lakeshore stretches 35 miles along Lake Michigan's eastern coastline. It also includes the North and South Manitou Islands. The park was established primarily for its outstanding natural features, including long beaches and dune formations. Tucked away on the southwest corner of South Manitou Island is a grove of white cedar trees. One of the fallen trees has 528 growth rings, dating its existence to before the arrival of Christopher Columbus. A 500-year-old cedar is still standing, making it the world's largest white cedar. The majestic tree spans 17 feet across and reaches 90 feet in height.

QUICK FACTS

Communication took on a new dimension in 1879. Detroit telephone users were the first to be given individual phone numbers.

Michigan's state song is "Michigan, My Michigan." The lyrics were written by Douglas Malloch.

On March 15, 1977, the Renaissance Center officially opened its riverfront office space. By 1987, an aerial train linked the center to Greektown and other downtown attractions.

The Renaissance Center is located in downtown Detroit, overlooking the Detroit River.

THE GREAT LAKES	Area (square miles)	Maximum Depth (feet)
Lake Superior	31,820	1,302
Lake Huron	23,010	750
Lake Michigan	22,178	923
Lake Erie	9,940	210
Lake Ontario	7,540	778

The Great Lakes are a significant natural resource for the United States, as well as the entire continent of North America. Together, the lakes contain about 20 percent of the world's fresh surface water. The Great Lakes also provide an important location for recreation, with about 10,500 miles of shoreline.

In many ways, water bodies define Michigan. About 40 percent of the state's total area of 96,705 square miles is comprised of the Great Lakes. Four of the five Great Lakes are located within Michigan, and residents are never more than 85 miles from the shore of a Great Lake. The Great Lakes make up the largest concentration of fresh water on the continent. In fact, Lake Superior is the largest freshwater lake in the world. With 3,288 miles of shoreline, Michigan is bordered by more water than the entire Atlantic coastline of the United States—only Alaska has a longer shoreline. The abundance of water in Michigan makes the state a great place for water sports enthusiasts, such as fishers, boaters, and swimmers.

Michigan has the longest freshwater shoreline in the world.

Sand dunes in the Lower Peninsula region have been created by westerly winds that blow off Lake Michigan.

QUICK FACTS

The record high temperature in Michigan was 112° Fahrenheit at Mio on July 13, 1936. The lowest recorded temperature was –51°F at Vanderbilt on February 9, 1934.

A cliff made of limestone rock, called the Niagara **Escarpment**, is found in the Upper Peninsula.

Mount Arvon is the highest point in the state. It towers 1,979 feet.

LAND AND CLIMATE

Glaciers shaped Michigan's two major land regions—the Great Lakes Plains and the Superior Uplands. The Great Lakes Plains covers the eastern half of the Upper Peninsula and the entire Lower Peninsula. This region is marked by swampland, sandstone **tablelands**, and fertile farmland. There are sand dunes along the western section of the Lower Peninsula.

The Superior Uplands are located in the western section of the Upper Peninsula. Fast flowing streams and waterfalls are found in this region, especially near Lake Superior. Lakes are also found in the Uplands. This area, the location of the Porcupine and Huron Mountains, is at a higher elevation than the rest of the state.

Winds blowing off the Great Lakes make for large snowfalls. Precipitation averages 26 to 36 inches per year. It is common to have snow piled as high as garage roofs in the Upper Peninsula. In December 2000, the state suffered a terrible snowstorm. A record 89.5 inches of snow fell.

Grand Haven, located along Michigan's coast, has seen many severe winter storms. The Grand Haven Lighthouse has withstood them all.

NATURAL RESOURCES

In the 1800s, when many parts of the country were in the midst of the gold boom, Michigan was experiencing a copper boom. Copper has traditionally been one of the top resources in the state. In the late 1800s, about half of the copper in the country came from Michigan. Copper mines on Keweenaw Peninsula extended 1 mile into the ground. By the 1900s, other states had discovered larger copper deposits. Michigan's deposits, however, remained the purest in the country.

Michigan is a leader in the production of magnesium, iron ore, gypsum, and peat. The state supplies about one-quarter of the iron ore required to make steel in the United States. The ore is formed into pellets that are used for blast-furnace steel making. Michigan is home to two large iron ore plants that produce more than 15 million tons of pellets every year. These pellets are shipped to major steel centers.

The Quincy Mine produced 726 million pounds of copper from 1856 to 1925.

QUICK FACTS

The biggest limestone **quarry** in the world is located near Rogers City.

Petoskey is the state stone. This coral fossil is found along Lake Michigan.

In 1997, oil and gas from Michigan earned about $865 million. That year, the state produced about 10 million barrels of oil and about 306 billion cubic feet of natural gas.

Salt is an important resource in Michigan. Large deposits are mined near Detroit. Salt is also obtained from salt water near Midland, Bay City, and Saginaw.

Port Calcite ships more than 10 million tons of limestone products to customers throughout the Great Lakes area each year.

The trillium, a forest wildflower, blooms from April to June in Michigan.

PLANTS AND ANIMALS

More than half of Michigan is forested, with forests consisting mainly of maple, birch, oak, and spruce trees. In the 1800s, many of the state's original forests were cleared for farming. Some original forests remain, however, such as a large stand found in Hartwick Pines State Park in the Lower Peninsula. Since the early 1900s, the state has made great efforts to rebuild its forests and to protect the **endangered** trees and plants found within them. Another hazard to forests—fires—has been greatly reduced by increasing public awareness of fire regulations and by the early detection of fires.

The trillium, a flower with three delicate petals, is protected by the Michigan government. Several types of trillium flowers, including the painted trillium, are on the state's endangered list. The painted trillium bears white flowers streaked with purple. Michiganders are not allowed to pick trilliums.

QUICK FACTS

The state wildflower, the dwarf lake iris, grows in the sand at Sleeping Bear Dunes.

The American chestnut tree can grow up to 100 feet tall. The trees are a valuable habitat for animals.

Throughout the state, wild raspberry, gooseberry, and elderberry shrubs bear delicious fruit.

The white pine is Michigan's official state tree.

Ferns and mosses grow in Michigan's swamp areas, as do cranberries.

Flowers that bloom in the summer include the daisy, iris, orange milkweed, rose, shooting star, and tiger lily.

Forests cover approximately 19.3 million acres of Michigan.

Michigan's state mammal is the white-tailed deer.

Unlike many zoos, the Detroit Zoo has open animal exhibits, which give the animals more freedom.

Conservationists count the number of warblers in an area by listening to their songs, which can be heard from a quarter of a mile away. Female warblers do not sing, so counters double the number of singers to come up with a total.

The robin is the official state bird, the brook trout is the official fish, and the painted turtle is the official reptile.

Isle Royale National Park covers 850 square miles and includes more than 200 tiny islands in Lake Superior. Michigan's only national park is dedicated to studying and preserving wildlife.

Michigan is home to a wide range of animals. Common state animals include deer, moose, bears, bobcats, and weasels. There are also some less common animals. The Kirtland's warbler is a rare North American bird. Michiganders have been working to save this endangered species for decades, with some success. A study in 2001 found there to be 1,085 male warblers in Michigan—200 more than the year prior. The total number of these birds, including female warblers, is about 2,170.

Kirtland's warblers inhabit only fourteen of Michigan's eighty-three counties today.

The threatened gray wolf and great antlered moose have grown in number, thanks to Isle Royale National Park in Lake Superior. For more than forty years, park officials have carefully studied the two species. In 1998, the wolf population had dropped to only fourteen, but by 2000, the number had jumped to twenty-nine. There are also about 850 moose on the island. Isle Royale is home to beavers, hares, foxes, bald eagles, and ospreys.

The Isle Royale National Park's gray wolf population grows and diminishes depending upon the population of its principal prey species, the moose.

The Henry Ford Museum is home to more than 1 million artifacts, 26 million documents, and about 80 historic structures.

TOURISM

Tourism in Michigan draws about 22 million visitors and billions of dollars to the state each year. Michigan is often associated with automobiles, but one of its tourist attractions does not even allow cars! Mackinac Island on Lake Huron offers a step back in time. With its shoreline measuring only 8.3 miles around, visitors can easily tour the island on a bicycle or horse. People can also hail a horse-drawn taxi.

Greenfield Village, founded by Henry Ford in 1929, is another top tourist attraction. It displays some interesting inventions. Greenfield Village features the home of airplane pioneers Orville and Wilbur Wright, as well as Thomas Edison's laboratories. While at Greenfield Village, people are sure to tour the Henry Ford Museum. It highlights national achievements in transportation, manufacturing, entertainment, and technology.

Dundee is home to a 225,000-square-foot retail phenomenon. Cabela's, which sells outdoor equipment, is no ordinary store. It has a large bronze sculpture at its entrance, a trout pond, a 40-foot mountain with a waterfall, and a gigantic aquarium. It draws about 6 million visitors each year.

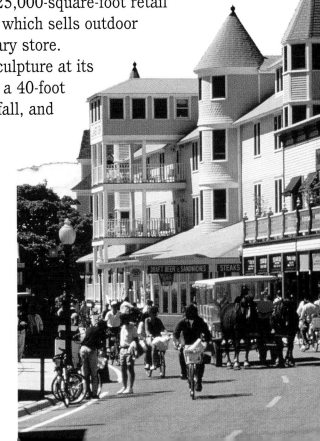

In 1898, the Village of Mackinac Island Council formally banned the use of motorized vehicles.

Worldwide, nearly 350,000 Ford employees go to work each day at offices, laboratories, or manufacturing facilities.

INDUSTRY

Detroit has long been known as the car capital of the world. The state manufactures more than one-quarter of the automobiles in the country. Ford, Chrysler, and General Motors established their headquarters around Detroit. The world headquarters of Ford in Dearborn displays the company's international links. Forty-two flags wave along the company driveway, representing the more than 30 countries in which Ford operates. Chrysler employs about 2,500 people in Michigan, and Detroit's 5.5-million-square-foot Renaissance Center was recently purchased by General Motors to serve as its world headquarters.

The construction industry is highly dependent upon Michigan's natural resources. Limestone, a rock found along the northern coast of the Lower Peninsula, is used in steel and portland cement. Michigan's sand and gravel deposits are also mined for construction purposes. Gypsum, used to make wallboard, **lath**, and plaster, is found in the Grand Rapids area and is quarried at Alabaster.

QUICK FACTS

The Great Lakes support some of the biggest boats used for freight. Ore carriers are 1,000 feet long.

Of the top 150 automotive suppliers in the United States, more than half are found in Michigan.

More than 580,000 Michiganders work in the auto industry. About 1 million people work in auto-related jobs. Combined, they represent about 30 percent of the state's work force.

Every year, an average of 10,000 passenger and cargo vessels pass through the Soo Locks. These locks are the world's largest waterway traffic system.

Michigan produces more sour cherries than any other state in the nation.

GOODS AND SERVICES

Much of Michigan's land is farmland. There are about 52,000 farms in Michigan, and they cover a third of the state. Farming brings approximately $37 billion to the state each year. Fruit is very important—the state is a key producer of cherries, apples, plums, strawberries, and grapes. Along with a variety of vegetables, some farmers also grow an edible **fungus**—the mushroom. In fact, about 17 million pounds of mushrooms are produced in Michigan each year. They are grown in special buildings with controlled temperature and humidity.

Michigan's economy relies on other kinds of manufacturing besides automobile manufacturing. While Grand Rapids is known for its cars, it is associated with furniture as well. The city has recently moved from low-cost to high-quality furniture production. Saginaw is a center for metal and glass manufacturing, and Muskegon is known for its billiard tables and bowling balls.

Young morel mushrooms are dried under direct sunlight for 8–10 hours. This ensures that the fungi will be preserved for years.

Michigan State University was the nation's first institution of higher learning to teach scientific agriculture.

Many people start their day off with a healthy breakfast thanks to Michigan's Kellogg brothers. In 1906, the Kellogg brothers worked together to invent nutritious foods for the patients at the Battle Creek **Sanitarium**. They flattened wheat berries into flakes, then baked them to add crispiness. So began the cold breakfast cereal industry. Battle Creek is still home to the Kellogg's Company headquarters, and Kellogg's yearly sales total more than $9 billion. An attraction at Kellogg's Cereal City, called "A Bowl Full of Fun," opened in June 1998. Visitors can discover how cereal is made and the history of the company in Battle Creek—a city that earned the nickname, "The Cereal Bowl of America."

After breakfast, many young Michiganders head off to school. Education is of great importance to the state of Michigan. It spends $7,166 each year on every student's education. This is $1,000 more per student than the national average. The state has forty-four public and sixty-six private post-secondary schools. Michigan State University, founded in 1855, is one of the largest universities in the United States.

Kellogg's Cereal City allows visitors to see how cereal is made with a re-creation of a cereal production line.

Birchbark canoes could be fashioned for a single person or for as many as fifty people. Canoes ranged from 10 to 24 feet in length.

FIRST NATIONS

It is estimated that there were Native Peoples living in the Michigan area as early as 10,000 years ago. Many of these people were members of the Chippewa, Menominee, Ottawa, Miami, and Potawatomi. These first groups hunted and fished, and later began to grow crops. The berries, herbs, and nuts that they gathered **supplemented** the corn, beans, squash, and other vegetables that they grew. They also took advantage of the large quantities of wild rice growing in the area. The forests of the Upper Peninsula gave the Native Peoples more than just valuable hunting ground. This area was rich in copper as well. Groups that lived in the Upper Peninsula about 5,000 years ago mined copper.

Michigan's Native Peoples created pottery with elaborate designs. They also made sturdy birchbark canoes, which were used for hunting and traveling. Groups traded food and goods with each other. By the 1600s, the Native Peoples had obtained a new trading partner—the French.

By the early 1600s, approximately 15,000 Native Americans lived in the Michigan area. About 12,000 of them lived in the southern portion of the Lower Peninsula.

QUICK FACTS

The Mound Builders, who lived in the Michigan area, gathered piles of earth for religious and burial grounds. A ceremonial center was discovered near present-day Grand Rapids.

The Potawatomi, Ojibwa, and the Ottawa shared common lifestyles and living areas.

Wild rice was so abundant in the Upper Peninsula that the Menominee did not have to grow any crops for food.

Although Samuel de Champlain sent many expeditions to North America, it was not until 1612 that he visited the eastern shores of Georgian Bay.

EXPLORERS AND MISSIONARIES

There was much European exploration along North America's waterways in the early 1600s. Many explorers were searching for the Northwest Passage—a direct route to the Pacific Ocean and the wealth of the Orient. Early explorers, many of whom were sent by Samuel de Champlain, the governor of New France (modern-day Canada), did not venture ashore. In 1619, a French explorer named Etienne Brulé became the first European to set foot in Michigan. Many French trappers and traders flocked to the area after Brulé's arrival. The French exchanged beads, pots, weapons, and clothing with Native Peoples for wolverine and beaver furs.

England also recognized the potential of the area. The English threatened the established and successful French operations. To protect themselves against English interference, the French colonized the territory. French soldiers and farmers built Fort Pontchartrain on the Detroit River in 1701. Many other forts were soon erected, but they did not prevent the English from capturing the area. They took Michigan during the French and Indian War, which was fought from 1754 to 1763.

Originally called Fort Pontchartrain du Detroit, the first permanent French settlement of the Detroit region was about 200 square feet. The English took control of it in 1760.

Father Jacques Marquette's Sault Ste. Marie is the third-oldest remaining settlement in the United States.

Explorers and traders were not the only people who were interested in coming to the Michigan area. Missionaries soon arrived as well. In 1660, Father René Ménard arrived at the tip of the Upper Peninsula. He founded a mission at Keweenaw Bay. Father Jacques Marquette spent more than one year studying Native-American languages so that he could communicate with the Native Peoples when he arrived. He established Michigan's first permanent settlement at Sault Ste. Marie in 1668 and then traveled to Wisconsin in 1669. Father Marquette quickly returned to Michigan when the Sioux forced him out of Wisconsin. Upon his return, he established another mission at Point Saint Ignace.

Missionary work in the area was difficult. Many priests and missionaries did not speak the languages, so they had trouble explaining their intentions. The cultural differences between the Native Peoples and the European missionaries also posed a problem. The missionaries' attempts to convert Native Peoples to Christianity were mostly unsuccessful in Michigan.

QUICK FACTS

By the early 1700s, forts, missions, and trading posts were spread across the Michigan area.

Father Jacques Marquette's mission at Sault Ste. Marie is the third-largest existing structure of its kind in the country.

European settlement of Michigan meant less space for the Native Peoples. Many groups, especially the Potawatomi, were forced out of Michigan and onto **reservations** in Oklahoma and Kansas.

In the seventeenth and eighteenth centuries, the fur trade relied upon the Great Lakes for the transport of precious furs.

Chief Pontiac of the Ottawas led the siege of Detroit. He was almost successful in capturing the fort.

EARLY SETTLERS

Once strongholds were built, such as Fort Michilimackinac on the Straits of Mackinac, the next step was settling the area. Hundreds of settlers from France were eager to live in Michigan. After France lost the French and Indian War, the English took over the fur trade. Rather than respecting the Native Peoples, the English mistreated them. This caused fighting and bloodshed. In the spring of 1763, an alliance of Native Americans, led by the Ottawa chief Pontiac, rebelled against the English. Pontiac led an attack on Detroit but failed to capture it. Just after defeating this uprising, the English had to quash the struggle for American independence. The American Revolution raged from 1775–1783. The English were unsuccessful. On January 11, 1805, President Thomas Jefferson signed an act creating the Michigan Territory, with Detroit as its capital.

In the early 1800s, many people were afraid to move to Michigan—they had heard that the dunes and swamps posed health hazards. In 1825, the new Erie Canal in New York made it easier to travel to the Michigan Territory and to see what it had to offer. Settlers began to arrive in great numbers. The population rose from 31,640 in 1830 to more than 212,000 just ten years later. In 1837, when Michigan's population reached 60,000, President Andrew Jackson signed the bill that made Michigan the twenty-sixth state.

By 1801, Detroit's population stood at about 600 residents.

QUICK FACTS

In 1820, there were about 9,000 settlers and 7,000 Native Peoples living in Michigan.

Most of Michigan's settlers in the 1830s came from New York and New England.

Chief Pontiac of the Ottawas rallied different Native Peoples together to fight against European control in 1763. They fought for control of Detroit for five months before withdrawing. This marked the last serious conflict between Michigan's Native Peoples and European settlers.

POPULATION

The waterfront city of Marquette covers a land area of 11.4 square miles.

Michigan's population grew steadily as it approached the twenty-first century. Between 1990 and 2000, the population increased by nearly 7 percent to bring the total up to 9.9 million. About 71 percent of Michiganders live in cities, and the population is most heavily concentrated in the Lower Peninsula. The state's largest city, Detroit, has more than 970,000 residents. Still, Detroit's population has declined dramatically since its peak of 1,850,000 in 1950. Nearly half of the state's population lives in the Detroit **metropolitan area**. By contrast, the largest Upper Peninsula city, Marquette, has fewer than 20,000 residents. In the northern part of the Upper Peninsula, there are more bears and deer than people.

The people in Michigan are from many different places around the world. Close to 14 percent of Michiganders are African American; this is higher than the national average of 12 percent. About 2.2 percent are Hispanic American. Asian and Pacific Islanders make up slightly more than 1 percent of the population. Native Americans make up 0.6 percent of the population, with most of them living on one of the seven state reservations.

QUICK FACTS

The third-largest suspension bridge in the country links people from the Upper and Lower Peninsulas. The bridge is 26,444 feet long and connects the cities of Saint Ignace in the north to Mackinaw City in the south.

After Detroit, Grand Rapids has the highest population in the state, with more than 185,000 people.

Upper Peninsula residents call themselves "Yoopers." This name began with the initials "UP," and became "Yoo-Pee," and then finally, "Yoopers."

Michigan has 1.4 million African-American residents.

The Great Seal of Michigan was chosen by the state's second governor, Lewis Cass. He based it on the art from the Hudson's Bay Fur Company seal. It was approved on June 2, 1835.

POLITICS AND GOVERNMENT

The Capitol building in Lansing is more than a government institution. It is also a stylish building. Hanging from the ceiling are nineteen copper, iron, and pewter **chandeliers**. No two are alike, as they were all specially designed by Tiffany's of New York. Each of these remarkable pieces weighs between 800 and 900 pounds.

The governor and lieutenant governor, along with other public servants such as the auditor general and the treasurer, are members of the executive branch. They each serve four-year terms. This branch is responsible for enforcing the state's laws.

The legislative branch is made up of the Senate and the House of Representatives. Thirty-eight Senators serve four-year terms, and 110 Representatives serve two-year terms. Representatives create new laws and change existing ones. The judicial branch consists of the state's courts. Michigan's highest court is the seven-member Supreme Court.

Michigan's Capitol, with its majestic dome, was built in Lansing in 1879.

Hart Plaza's annual Mexican Fiesta features Hispanic foods, music, and art. At the festival, vendors sell their pottery, furniture, and jewelry.

CULTURAL GROUPS

Many people of different cultures call Michigan home, including people of German, Polish, and Irish ancestry. Many people from the Middle East also live in the state. In 1919, the United States' first **mosque** was built in Highland Park. Arab Americans in the area still use the mosque. With more than 300,000 Arab Americans, the Detroit metropolitan area has the country's largest Arab-American community in the nation.

The African-American population in Michigan is also large, especially in Detroit. About 75 percent of the city's population is African American. Many of the city's residents celebrate African-American culture through events such as the African World Festival, which is held every August. More than 1.5 million people attend this festival to enjoy African-American art, food, displays, and activities. The Museum of African-American History in Detroit highlights the achievements and contributions of African Americans to the state and the country. It is the largest museum of its kind in the world.

Three local Detroit artists sculpted the *Tight Pack Figures* statue, which honors the Africans who were enslaved and put on ships bound for North America.

Frankenmuth's Bavarian Festival, first held in 1959, draws more than 80,000 people each year.

Some Michiganders came to the United States from the Netherlands. There is even a city named after their country of origin. Dutch Americans celebrate their culture during the Tulip Time Festival in Holland, Michigan. This ten-day event in May features a parade, fireworks, Klompen dancing, and traditional attire, such as clogs. The Dutch village re-creates the way a town in the Netherlands would have looked 100 years ago.

In the city of Frankenmuth, the German culture is prominent. The city's nickname, "Michigan's Little Bavaria," is fitting. Frankenmuth, which resembles a German village, is the site of the annual Bavarian Festival. This event is celebrated in June with German bands, parades, and plenty of bratwurst sausage and Bavarian pretzels. During the festival, rides modeled after those at the Munich Oktoberfest grounds in Germany are sure to thrill attendees.

Stevie Wonder has been blind since birth. That did not prevent him from becoming a musician—he started playing piano when he was only four years old.

ARTS AND ENTERTAINMENT

Michigan has a vibrant art community. There are many art museums and galleries found throughout the state, including the DeWaters Art Center and the Kalamazoo Institute of Arts. Illustrator and children's writer Chris Van Allsburg from Grand Rapids has won several awards, including the Caldecott Award, for his illustrations in such books as *Jumanji* and *The Polar Express*.

Michigan has played a large role in the United States' music scene. Detroit is home to the original Motown Records studios. It was the first record company to feature African-American musicians. Great musicians, including The Supremes, Michael Jackson, and Stevie Wonder began their careers with Motown.

Stevie Wonder, born in Saginaw, recorded his first song when he was thirteen years old in Detroit. Since that time, he has won many Grammy Awards and has produced numerous hit songs, including "I Just Called to Say I Love You" and "Ebony and Ivory."

QUICK FACTS

Three million people participate in the Detroit Festival of the Arts every September. The festival presents arts and crafts shows and musical, dance, and theater productions.

Leonardo da Vinci's 24-foot sculpture of a horse, called *Il Gavallo*, stands in Grand Rapids.

The Supremes were one of the most successful female musical groups of the sixties, with twelve #1 pop singles, several gold recordings, and many sold-out concerts.

Before Harrison Ford took the part, Tom Selleck was offered the role of Indiana Jones in the film *Raiders of the Lost Ark*.

Madonna is one of Michigan's most famous celebrities. This singer, dancer, and actress was born in Bay City in 1958. Her first album, simply titled *Madonna*, was a smash success thanks to her new pop sound and flashy fashion style. She has since released many successful albums including *Like a Prayer* and *Ray of Light*. Madonna's fame has taken her to Hollywood. She has acted in many movies, including *Evita*, *Dick Tracy*, and *A League of Their Own*.

Many other talented Hollywood entertainers hail from Michigan. Detroit native Tom Selleck starred as Thomas Magnum on the 1980s television series Magnum, P. I. The show aired for eight seasons and won Selleck an Emmy Award in 1984. Selleck brought attention to his hometown by wearing a Detroit Tigers baseball cap in many of the episodes. He has also enjoyed a successful film career, having starred in such movies as *Three Men and a Baby* and *Mr. Baseball*. Selleck has also guest starred on the television sitcom *Friends*.

QUICK FACTS

Detroit's Diana Ross became a music **diva** as the lead singer of The Supremes. She has also enjoyed a successful solo career.

Francis Ford Coppola is from Detroit. He won an Academy Award for directing *The Godfather II*.

Zany Detroit native Gilda Radner was one of the original Saturday Night Live comedians.

The Interlochen Arts Academy near Traverse City teaches students in grades 9–12 about music, theater, and creative writing.

Madonna earned a dance scholarship to the University of Michigan but left after two years to become a musician.

SPORTS

Copper Peak boasts a ski jump that stands 241 feet above Chippewa Hill.

From swimming to skiing, there is a sport for everyone in Michigan. Organizations, such as the Michigan Mountain Biking Association, lead members through the state with pedal power. Running is another popular pastime, and there are many running groups in Michigan. Some train for the Crim 10-mile Race in Flint.

For those looking to enjoy the outdoors at a slower pace, golf is the perfect sport. The north-central part of Michigan is known as "America's Summer Golf Capital." There are twenty world-championship golf courses in this area and ten golf resorts. In 1996, the state welcomed thirty-four new golf courses, more than any other state in the country.

In winter, sporty Michiganders can tackle the slopes at one of the fifty-seven ski resorts in the state. Adventurous skiers can try ski flying, or ski jumping. After gliding off a flight deck, ski jumpers can soar for hundreds of feet before returning to the ground. For those who prefer flatter surfaces, Michigan offers about 8,000 miles of cross-country ski trails.

The Detroit Tigers were once called the Wolverines, but they changed their name after a sports writer noted that the team's striped socks resembled tiger paws.

QUICK FACTS

The Porcupine and Huron Mountains receive large amounts of snow during the winter months. This makes for fantastic skiing.

The many waterways lure swimmers, fishers, and boaters to Michigan each year.

Marquette is a training location for twenty-three different Olympic events.

Ali Hoxie is a Michigan snowboard champion. At 18 years of age, she won the U.S. Amateur Snowboard Association Nationals.

With more than forty downhill ski resorts and more than 2,113 miles of groomed cross-country trails, Michigan is a skier's paradise.

At 6 feet 9 inches, Earvin "Magic" Johnson is the tallest guard in NBA history.

QUICK FACTS

Detroit's Joe Louis
was one of the best boxers in history. He became the heavyweight champion in 1937 and defended his title for twelve years. When he retired in 1951, he had claimed sixty-six wins in seventy-one fights.

There are many professional sports teams to keep Michiganders cheering. Major League Baseball's Detroit Tigers have been in the league since 1901. Over the years, the Tigers have won four World Series Championships and have competed in five others. In football, the Detroit Lions battled their way to the NFL playoffs six times in the 1990s. Lions running back Barry Sanders tied for the Most Valuable Player Award in the 1997–1998 season. In hockey, the Detroit Red Wings have amazed fans since 1926. Between 1948 and 1955, the team won four Stanley Cup championships.

The Detroit Pistons of the National Basketball Association draw huge crowds. The Pistons won the NBA Championship in 1989 and 1990. Also, the Women's National Basketball Association added the Detroit Shock in 1998.

A magical basketball superstar hails from the Wolverine State. Earvin "Magic" Johnson was born in Lansing. He made his name on the basketball court as one of the Los Angeles Lakers' best guards. Magic Johnson transformed the game of basketball with his no-look passing and his fast-break style. His winning smile, along with his fantastic athletic abilities, earned him instant star status.

The Detroit Red Wings pleased their hockey fans when they became the Stanley Cup champions of 1997 and 1998.

Brain Teasers

1 How much did Henry Ford's Model T car sell for in the early 1900s?

Answer: The car cost $290 in 1925, which meant that more people could afford an automobile. Cars were no longer just for the wealthy.

2 How many flags have flown over Michigan?

Answer: Four. They are the French, English, Spanish, and United States flags.

4 Which automotive firsts took place in Michigan?

Answer: The first mile of concrete highway was completed in 1909, and Henry Ford's assembly lines first rolled in 1913.

3 Which city boasts the world's biggest cherry pie?

Answer: Traverse City. On July 25, 1987, bakers made a 28,355-pound pie that was 17.5 feet across and 26 inches deep. The pie tin is on display near the Traverse City marina.

5

How did the Sleeping Bear Dune get its name?

Answer: A Native-American legend says that a bear and her two cubs were swimming across Lake Michigan to escape a forest fire. The cubs were not strong enough to make the trip and drowned. The mother was sad and tired when she reached the shore, and she laid down to wait for her cubs. The gods felt sorry for the bear and covered her with sand.

6

Who was Brigadier General George Custer?

Answer: Brigadier General George Custer led the Michigan Brigade, a regiment fighting against the rebels during the Civil War. Custer received the rebel leader's towel as a sign of surrender. After the war, the Monroe native led soldiers in the frontier fight with the Native Peoples. Custer's group attacked at Little Bighorn. Custer underestimated the strength of the Native Peoples, and he and his troops were killed.

7

What delicious drink was "accidentally" invented in Michigan?

Answer: Vernors ginger ale was created in Detroit. In 1862, pharmacist James Vernor was in the midst of creating a new beverage when he was called away to serve in the American Civil War. He returned four years later to find that the drink he had stored in an oak case had acquired a delicious gingery flavor.

8

Michigan has a religious claim-to-fame. What is it?

Answer: Indian River has the largest crucifix in the world. It is called Cross in the Woods.

FOR MORE INFORMATION

Books

Aylesworth, Thomas G., *Eastern Great Lakes*. Chelsea House Publishers, 1988.

Leacock, Elspeth, *The Midwest*. Washington, DC: National Geographic Society, 2002.

Lloyd, Tanya, *Michigan*. New York: Whitecap Books, 2000.

Sirvaitis, Karen, *Michigan*. Minneapolis: Lerner Publications Co., 1994.

Web Sites

You can also go online and have a look at the following Web sites:

50 States: Michigan
www.50states.com/michigan.htm

Tourism Michigan
www.travel.michigan.org

Detroit Tigers
http://tigers.mlb.com/NASApp/mlb/det/homepage/det_homepage.jsp

The Tulip Time Festival
www.holland.org

Some Web sites stay current longer than others. To find other Michigan Web sites, enter search terms such as "Detroit," "Bay City," "Lansing," or any other topic you want to research.

GLOSSARY

carillon: a set of bells, usually hanging in a tower, that are rung either mechanically or manually

chandeliers: ornamental hanging light fixtures that hold several lights

diva: a great female singer and celebrity

endangered: at risk

escarpment: a steep slope at the edge of a plateau

fungus: an organism that lives by decomposing and absorbing the organic material in which it grows

lath: a thin, narrow strip of wood

metropolitan area: a large city and its surrounding communities

mosque: a Muslim temple or place of worship

peninsulas: pieces of land that are almost entirely surrounded by water

quarry: an open pit for mining resources such as stone and gravel

reservations: areas of land set aside by the government for Native Americans

sanitarium: a health resort

supplemented: completed or added to

tablelands: a large region of elevated, flat land

INDEX